SHUTTING DOWN BULLIES

SHUTTING DOWN

CYBERBULLIES

Pam T. Glaser and Judy Monroe Peterson

rosen publishing's
rosen
central

New York

Published in 2020 by The Rosen Publishing Group, Inc.
29 East 21st Street, New York, NY 10010

Copyright © 2020 by The Rosen Publishing Group, Inc.

First Edition

Library of Congress Cataloging-in-Publication Data

Names: Glaser, Pam T., author. | Peterson, Judy Monroe, author.
Title: Shutting down cyberbullies / Pam T. Glaser and Judy Monroe Peterson.
Description: New York : Rosen Publishing, 2020 | Series: Shutting down bullies |
Audience: Grades 5–8. | Includes bibliographical references and index.
Identifiers: LCCN 2019015037| ISBN 9781725346925 (library bound) | ISBN 9781725346918 (pbk.)
Subjects: LCSH: Cyberbullying—Juvenile literature. |
Cyberbullying—Prevention—Juvenile literature.
Classification: LCC HV6773.15.C92 G53 2020 | DDC 302.34/3—dc23
LC record available at https://lccn.loc.gov/2019015037

Manufactured in the United States of America

Some of the images in this book illustrate individuals who are models.
The depictions do not imply actual situations or events.

CONTENTS

Introduction

Before technology evolved to where people could communicate with a few taps on a handheld electronic device, bullies were classmates or cousins. You could get bullied on the bus home from school or during recess. But bullies were limited to the people kids saw every day. Technology, however, has not only opened the world up to a wider circle of communication, it's also opened young people up to new ways of bullying and being bullied. Any type of bullying that occurs via an electronic device, social media, or an online forum is considered cyberbullying.

Cyberbullying isn't limited to hurtful words and actions either. This type of bullying can include sharing of personal info meant to embarrass another person, like a low test score, a personal conversation, a video, or a humiliating picture of someone. Once something appears online, it's very hard to get rid of it. Take, for instance, the woman who would become known as the Ermahgerd girl, Maggie Goldenberger. Back when Maggie and a friend were in their early teens, they would dress up and take Polaroids of themselves as characters they had created. Maggie posed for a photo of herself in character as a girl with pigtails making a silly face while holding up some *Goosebumps* books. Later, she posted the photo on her MySpace page because she still loved it. She didn't think much about it, but years later, she discovered that a Canadian teenager had spotted the photo and posted it to a more mainstream site. Others downloaded the photo and Photoshopped in funny things for "Ermahgerd girl" to say. Pretty soon, the picture was everywhere. Luckily for her, the meme was all in good fun and she didn't suffer any long-term effects from her picture going viral. But what if the image that gets passed around is one that shows someone in a compromising position? In 2014, actress Jennifer Lawrence and a number of other female

Modern teens often rely on communication via social media or text, making them vulnerable to cyberbullies.

celebrities were hacked and had personal, intimate photos posted online by a group of hackers. The photos were posted on online forums like 4chan and Reddit, where they could be easily downloaded. Although the photos were eventually taken down by the moderators, nothing can ever erase them permanently. In this case, the victims didn't even know their bullies personally. A cyberbully can be a total stranger who lives on the other side of the world from a victim.

Around 15.5 percent of high school students have experienced cyberbullying, according to the National Bullying Prevention Center. If you've experienced cyberbullying or know someone who has, it can be helpful to understand more about why this happens, how you can break the cycle of bullying, and how to get help with some of the long-term effects of this type of abuse.

CHAPTER ONE

Victims of cyberbullies

Cyberbullying can be a lot scarier than traditional forms of bullying because victims begin to feel unsafe everywhere. The victim of a school bully knows that at the end of the day, he or she can go home. But a cyberbully can invade a person's life in more ways than one and at any time. And if a victim doesn't know a cyberbully personally, it's impossible to know that bully's limits. Will the bully be satisfied with just sending harassing text messages, or could he or she be capable of greater measures of harm? Victims of cyberbullying often feel angry, embarrassed, or unsafe. They may become depressed

A lot of teens will feel isolation and insecurity as a result of bullying. They might stop feeling safe anywhere.

depressed and isolated and experience hopelessness, helplessness, and sadness. Cyberbullying can affect friendships and family relationships. A victim might be afraid to reach out for help or talk about what's happening to him or her.

THE EMOTIONAL TOLL

Victims who are afraid or depressed can struggle with concentration and not do well on homework and tests. As a result, their grades might drop. Others might have problems falling or staying asleep, have headaches or stomachaches, or get sick often. Sometimes, they gain or lose weight. Some cyberbullying targets feel anxious and jumpy. They might shake and sweat and their heart might pound.

Many targets may feel stressed when receiving emails or text messages or when participating in an online game. Some may avoid checking email or social media. Other victims will not talk about their online activity with anyone.

Some targets of cyberbullying drop out of school activities or sports teams or stop going to school. They may lose interest in hobbies and friends, have low energy, and have trouble making decisions. Those who are depressed might abuse alcohol or other drugs or drive recklessly. Sometimes, victims need to change schools to escape their cyberbullies. In extreme cases, particular targets may feel the only way out of depression is to commit suicide.

Girls are more frequently involved in cases of cyberbullying than boys because they're often less directly confrontational.

BEING A TARGET

Young people being mean to one another with electronic devices may begin as early as the second grade. The average age of a cyberbully victim is 15. Girls are more likely to be targets than boys, and older girls receive more online threats than older boys.

Teens who are different in some way or have behaviors that others find annoying or amusing are likely to become victims of cyberbullying. Victims may have low self-esteem and feel insecure. Some may not have the social skills and the ability to communicate to stop cyberbullying or get help. Many victims are not assertive or do not know how to stand up for themselves. For example, some teens feel they will be tattling and get someone in trouble if they report cyberbullying.

The more time teens spend on the internet, the more likely they are to experience cyberbullying. Online activities include getting and sending texts or emails, using Facebook or Twitter, sharing photos on Instagram, building websites, or online gaming.

Sometimes, targets fight back by striking out at their cyberbullies. They might fire off angry emails or post nasty comments on chat forums, Facebook, or Twitter. Then they become bullies themselves. Cyberbullying can escalate quickly. Responding in anger sometimes only creates new bullies.

BULLIES ONLINE

Any type of bullying or harassment that occurs online or via cell phone or other electronic device is considered cyberbullying. A common type of cyberbullying is sending mean or threatening emails, direct messages, or texts to hurt someone. Some teens may also take private messages and forward them to others or post them on websites or in a group chat to embarrass another person. They might share conversations with others without permission or create insulting websites or fake social media profiles. Numerous bullies use social media to spread rumors, insults, and lies or to make fun of somebody. Cyberbullies may post embarrassing photos or videos of their targets on social media.

Some teens have more than one account on social networks. They may use one to interact with family and relatives and another one to bully people. Others might create a fake online person to trick people into telling them personal information. For example, a shy boy might not know that an online acquaintance is really a bully and confide that he has a crush on a popular girl. The bully could then forward this information for others to read. Some bullies might hack into a teen's profile and pretend to be that teen to cause problems. These cyberbullies might spread lies about someone to make that person look bad or get in trouble.

Bullying can cross the line into harassment, including cyber threats and cyberstalking. Threatening to harm someone is a cyber threat. Criminal laws against making cyber threats are in place. Cyberstalking is repeated harassment, such as using the internet to follow and observe someone in a threatening way, which causes the victim to feel fearful.

People cyberbully for many reasons. It can be teasing that gets out of hand and turns into taunts and jeers. A grudge held by a victim might turn into revenge. Peer pressure might cause someone to step into the role of cyberbully. Some teen cyberbullies might mimic cruel behavior they see in a movie, TV show, or video on YouTube, or have experienced cyberbullying themselves. Other teens use social media to deliberately hurt someone with their words or actions.

PLAYING GAMES ONLINE

Many teens enjoy online multiplayer or interactive gaming. But gaming forums often attract cyberbullies, who might taunt and tease players at lower skill levels. They might harass or abuse female or LGBTQ players. They may continue to bother someone who has responded to their initial attacks or pretend to be someone else and make up lies about teens or other gamers.

BULLYING AND TWITTER

Since it was introduced to the public in 2007, Twitter has become a popular go-to for sharing ideas, promoting work, talking politics, and keeping in touch with friends. But since many users post to Twitter under their online identities, it can be difficult to know if the person who just started following you is a real person who shares your interests or an online troll waiting to respond to your posts with vitriol. If you find yourself dealing with a Twitter troll, try the following:

1. Unfollow and block anyone who makes you uncomfortable, even if what that user is saying doesn't violate Twitter's terms of use. It's okay to protect yourself.

2. If the harassment continues, file a report with Twitter.

3. If a troll threatens you with violence, report the user to Twitter and keep documentation of the abuse on file. You might need to show proof of harassment.

4. Log off and take a break. Go spend time with friends and loved ones.

5. Be there for other Twitter users facing abuse or harassment. You can report harassment on another person's behalf.

Twitter can often make it a little diffcult to escape from cyberbullies. It's important to know your rights and how to protect yourself.

LEAVING OTHERS OUT

A teen can be bullied without directly interacting with the bully. For example, a cyberbully might delete a teen from a friend's buddy list to make that teen feel left out. Or a bully can lock someone out from everyone's messaging servers. The excluded person feels degraded and alone because of being isolated from the others.

Online gaming gives some bullies a place to victimize others anonymously.

A cyberbully might exclude teens from a group on Facebook or block them on Instagram, Twitter, or other social networking sites. Bullies then build a community in which its members know what is going on in the victim's life. They might post hurtful messages, pictures, or videos about the teen victim.

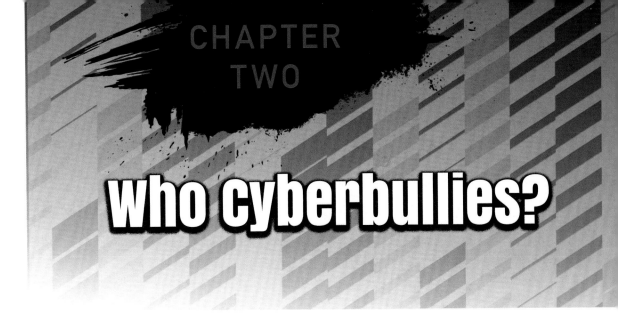

CHAPTER TWO

Who Cyberbullies?

Every cyberbully has a reason for being a bully, even if he or she doesn't understand the reason. Some may have low self-esteem and think being a bully will help them feel better. Cyberbullies want to upset, hurt, or scare other people to feel superior and powerful. They want power over people at any cost, or they seek a sense of control and attention by striking out at others. Reaching out via electronic devices or social media allows them to reach their targets at any time. These devices can also provide bullies with a wider audience than only the target.

WHAT MAKES A CYBERBULLY?

Exactly who is a cyberbully is somewhat unknown because there is no single accepted definition of cyberbullying in the United States. In addition, many people remain anonymous until caught. They can hide their identities by using temporary email accounts or social media profiles that allow them to remain anonymous.

Smartphones allow users to make calls, text, game, and use social media apps. They're amazing devices but can make cyberbullying easier.

The cyberbullies are then faceless, and victims can't see their real names or contact information.

Cyberbullies are often preteens and teens, although they can be people of any age. If savvy with technology, they can remain hidden while harming others. Most cyberbullies know their victims either in person or online. The target may be a classmate, a current or former friend, a relative, and so on. Some cyberbullies become familiar with their targets from forums or online games.

People might cross the line with something they write or show on social media or send to a group of friends. Sometimes, what one person thinks is a joke could be insulting to someone else.

A number of factors or situations can increase the risk of a teen becoming a cyberbully. However, having one or more of these does not always mean that a teen will become a bully. Some factors that can have an effect include having poor self-control and feeling that it is okay to be cruel or violent, perhaps

#GAMERGATE

In 2014, a group of gamers got upset with a video game developer named Zoe Quinn over a game she had created called *Depression Quest*. Quinn's text-based game took players through her own experiences with depression. They didn't like that Quinn was a female developer in a field that had always been dominated by men. A former boyfriend of Quinn's got involved, alleging that she had cheated on him and therefore deserved revenge. Angry gamers started sending Quinn harassing messages accusing her of having a relationship with a video game journalist to get good reviews for *Depression Quest*. The harassment evolved into death threats. A feminist critic named Anita Sarkeesian made a video speaking out against this kind of abuse and threats against women. Soon, Sarkeesian was receiving threats as well. Both women were afraid for their lives and forced to move out of their homes. While the controversy eventually died down, similar issues have occurred in the comic book industry and other male-dominated fields of entertainment as well.

from examples set at home in the family. Abusing others is a way for some cyberbullies to cope with difficult situations at home, school, or work.

BYSTANDERS

Bystanders are not bullies or victims, but they witness cyberbullying taking place. They may know it is wrong but do not take any action to stop the bully or to help the victim. By their inaction, they give approval for the cyberbully to continue his

Breakups and the ends of friendships often result in bullying situations. When people are angry and upset, they often act irrationally.

or her improper behavior. For example, teens might participate in a group text in which abusive language is being used against another person. Whether they add their own comments or say nothing at all, such actions encourage the bully who originally sent the messages. Other teens read rude and personal emails and texts or look at embarrassing photos of someone but do not pass them on. However, by doing nothing, bystanders are part of the cyberbullying and are not being respectful and kind to the victims.

Many bystanders to cyberbullying do not feel good about themselves and can become troubled or sad. The bystanders, the bully, and the victim all experience harm in some way when cyberbullying occurs.

ELECTRONIC DEVICES AND CYBERBULLYING

Understanding how cyberbullies work can help many teens deal with a bully. Cyberbullies do not physically hit or kick their targets. Using technology, they hurt people's feelings and make them feel unsafe and scared. When people think they cannot be seen or found out online, they may do things they would never do in person. Some teens mistakenly believe that bullying online is nothing serious. The ease of cyberbullying may appeal to them. People can instantly send out put-downs, rumors, gossip, and embarrassing photos in emails, social media, group texts, or online forums. For example, a girl might send a stream of nasty text messages to her former boyfriend after a painful breakup. Other people might use editing software to change electronic photos or videos to show something about an individual that is embarrassing or untrue. With a few clicks, one person can post hurtful words or pictures to a few or thousands of viewers.

Some cyberbullies know that using the internet can make it difficult to trace and find them. Computers can easily allow people to be anonymous, enabling bullies to hurt their victims without seeing them in person. In addition, many teens are not supervised by adults when using the internet or cell phones. This lack of attention can lead cyberbullies to feel that they can be hurtful to their victims and will not get caught by their parents or authorities.

By using electronic devices, bullies can get to teens at home, including evenings and weekends. They can attack repeatedly. Even if a bully stops, it may be difficult or impossible to remove all the mean online electronic messages or photos. Cyberbullies may not take down cruel photos or posts when asked to do so.

GENDERED CYBERBULLYING

Female and male teens tend to cyberbully in different ways. Female cyberbullies prefer to share personal information about their targets. They are more likely to write mean and upsetting messages. By spreading rumors and gossip, they can damage another teen's social life. Girls who bully often harass victims privately, through social media or via text.

Male cyberbullies more often make direct threats online to get revenge on someone else. They are more apt to tease and call their target names one on one. Boys typically cyberbully openly, on social media or via group text. They might hack into a victim's computer and steal passwords. They might use electronic devices to pass around hurtful photos, drawings, or other images of their targets. Boys, more often than girls, use exclusion to cyberbully.

VICTIMS IN HARM'S WAY

All forms of cyberbullying are harmful to victims. Teens feel they cannot hide or have no way to escape from cyberbullies, even at home. They can be attacked online day or night, and they might not know what is being said about them or who is behind the cyberbullying. Targets might fear for their safety because of continual online threats and harassment.

Repeated bullying can cause victims to feel tense, afraid, and

Depression is a common result of cyberbullying. Isolation and constant fear for one's safety can leave a person feeling hopeless.

anxious. Teen victims might have more health problems, such as headaches, stomachaches, and colds. They can have mood difficulties and be hostile, angry, or irritable. Some cry often and easily. The self-esteem of victims may decrease, leading to feelings of worthlessness.

Some targets do not report cyberbullying and keep their problem a secret. They think they can handle the taunts and

19

teasing themselves. Some feel weak and unpopular or are too embarrassed to speak up. Sometimes, they think they have done something wrong and worry they will be punished. Victims may fear revenge from their bullies. Another concern is that adults will not take their complaints seriously or will react in upsetting ways, such as taking away their electronic devices.

Such secrecy can make teens feel alone or isolated. The effects might be long-lasting and can include depression, anxiety, drug abuse, and abuse of family members. Targets of cyberbullying may withdraw and drop out of school activities, clubs, or sports teams, or not want to go to school. They lose interest in hobbies and friends, have low energy, and have difficulty concentrating and making decisions. Victims of cyberbullying might react by arriving at school very late or very early and avoiding school or activities. Sometimes, teen victims run away from home. Others feel that the only way out of their depression is to commit suicide.

MYTHS AND FACTS ABOUT BULLYING

Myth: Cyberbullying is a more common occurrence for young people than in-person bullying.

Fact: While 15 percent of teens say they have been cyberbullied, between 25 and 33 percent of teens have dealt with in-person bullying.

Myth: Anonymity in bullying began with online communication.

Fact: Social media and other forms of online communication certainly contribute to anonymity for bullies, but long before the internet was invented, bullies passed anonymous notes, scrawled comments about a victim on a wall, or found other ways to be cruel without giving their identities away.

Myth: Cyberbullying alone is causing increasing rates of teen suicide.

Fact: Experts are still trying to learn as much as possible about the link between cyberbullying and suicide. They believe that bullying and harassment are extremely damaging and can trigger underlying issues with mental illness, depression, or anxiety in teens. Cyberbullying can also add to already existing feelings of stress or loneliness, which is common for a lot of teens. Bottom line: if you're struggling with suicidal thoughts, reach out to a parent or trusted adult as soon as possible.

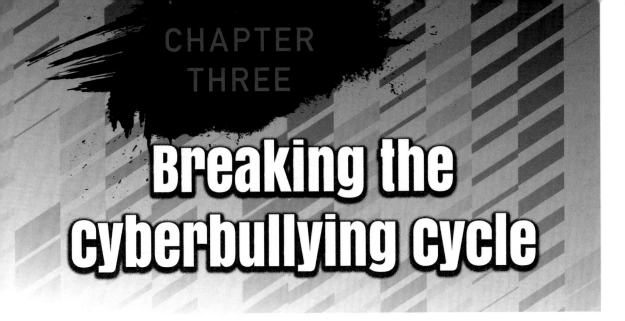

CHAPTER THREE

Breaking the Cyberbullying Cycle

Protecting yourself or a friend from a cyberbully can be really scary and difficult, but it is possible to get some help breaking the cycle of cyberbullying. It might help to sit down and make a plan. Many people feel upset or scared while online, but you can take action to stop the bullies, including asking for help. Teens should be open to getting help and can also help others who are being cyberbullied.

AVOIDING BEING BULLIED ALTOGETHER

Being careful while online is important for everyone. Cyberbullies can reach people only if they know how to find them. Teens should not give out personal information, such as passwords, to anyone online, not even a friend. Someone who can get or guess a password can then pose as that teen. Only parents or another trusted adult should know a teen's passwords. Many teens change their passwords regularly.

Other personal information that no one online should see include physical descriptions or photographs, phone number, addresss, birth dates, Social Security numbers, driver's license numbers, school names, or bank and credit card numbers. Teens probably should not open emails or messages from people they do not know. It could be spam, which might contain upsetting messages or even viruses or other types of malware. If teens decide to message or chat with someone they do not know, they should not share their age, address, or any other personal information.

Social media networks like Facebook, Twitter, and Instagram allow teens to set up a profile to offer information

Talking to a parent or other trusted adult can do a lot to help a teen work through some issues and develop a plan for escaping the cycle of bullying.

about themselves. Teens should not enter their age, phone number, home address, or school on their profile or other postings. They can choose an icon to use for profiles instead of posting personal photos. Online social networking, email, and instant messaging sites allow teens to set limits on the people they can chat or message with by using privacy settings. Some online games also have privacy settings.

Teens need to be careful about the people they put on their friends and buddy lists. Friends can save, copy, rewrite, and repost whatever teens put on a social networking site, online forum, or other website. Always check with your friends before sharing images of them online.

A GOOD, STRONG PASSWORD

Many email, social network, and gaming sites ask people to choose a username and password. Having usernames and passwords that others cannot easily guess can help protect against cyberbullies. Teens should not use their real names as their usernames because everyone on a site can see usernames.

A strong password is eight to sixteen characters in length and includes lowercase and uppercase letters, numbers, punctuation marks, and other characters. Avoid passwords based on dictionary terms, usernames, relative or pet names, telephone numbers, birthdays, and other information that may be readily known or easy to guess. To create a password, some teens think of an uncommon phrase or short sentence and take the first, second, or last letter of each word. They turn these letters into their password by adding special characters near the beginning, middle, or end of the letters. Words, letters, or characters should not be repeated in a row, such as in the passwords "deskdesk" or "11B2wtt." Some sites will tell you how strong a password is when you're creating one. Keep yourself safe by frequently updating your password using these rules.

Logging off and spending some quality time with family will help remind you that you aren't alone and people do care about you.

If teens think that someone else knows their password, they should change it right away. People should not write down and keep their passwords where others can easily find them.

HOW TO RESPOND

People deal with cyberbullying in different ways. Sometimes, they can take care of the cyberbullying on their own by ignoring the bully or deleting the bully's messages without reading them. Some cyberbullies give up if they don't get a response. Another option is to log off from social media or shut down your electronic device and just take a break. Changing usernames, email addresses, or passwords might keep a bully away. You can often block unwanted phone numbers from all your devices easily. Limiting screen time is another good step. If harassment by phone or text doesn't stop, it might be time to change your phone number.

You can also block a bully who is harassing you via email or social media. Unfollow and block anyone who makes you feel unsafe or uncomfortable. File a report with the social networking site if the harassment continues. Don't open any emails or messages from people you don't know.

REACHING OUT FOR HELP

Some cyberbullies will not back down, causing teens to feel scared or distressed. However, they are not alone and can get help. Telling someone is important. Teens can tell a parent or another trusted adult, such as a relative, teacher, coach, guidance counselor, or youth group leader. People should never be afraid to speak up or feel cyberbullying is their fault. Teens should be honest about their experiences and any steps they have taken to deal with the bullies.

Victims should not respond to cyberbullies. Instead, they should save any abusive or nasty emails or messages. Take screen grabs of the harassment and file them away just in case you need them later. Make sure you keep track of dates and times that the harassment occurred. Forward the collected abuse to someone you trust for safekeeping. Recording the names of everyone who sends bullying messages is important because cyberbullies sometimes use several names.

CYBERBULLYING AT SCHOOL

If cyberbullied at school, students should report it. There might be a bullying box for reporting such incidents available at school. Students can explain the problem even when they do not know or want to say who the bullies are. Some schools

Sometimes the best course of action is to not respond to bullies at all, just walk away and ignore them. If things escalate beyond that, it's time to ask for help.

have a bullying court that deals with bullying. Teachers and other staff members are usually not involved. Many schools have antibullying policies and rules that discuss how the school will deal with acts of bullying. The policy is available for all students at school and may also be available to read online. Guidance counselors are a good resource. They are trained to deal with bullying online, in school, and on school grounds.

REPORTING HARASSMENT TO PROVIDERS

Bullies sometimes use fake email addresses to hide their true identities, so if you're receiving harassing emails, file a report with that provider, such as Gmail or Mail.com. Block users and report any harassment that comes in via social media. Online multiplayer games often have options for reporting harassment as well. Read up on the harassment policies of sites that you use to see if someone is violating them.

HANDLING GAMER BULLIES

If bullies strike during online gaming, report the harassment to the game's developers. There are sometimes in-game options for doing this so you don't have to lose too much time away from the game. You might also be able to reach out via email or social media if the harassment

Video game developer Brianna Wu was the target of online harassment as a result of Gamergate, to the point where she feared for her safety.

continues or seems to show evidence of a wider problem with the game. You might also consider setting up a group play that includes only trusted friends. If you find yourself getting overwhelmed, log off and take a break.

ENDING TEXT AND PHONE HARASSMENT

Bullying by phone can take the form of nasty or silent phone calls or mean text messages. Don't answer a call from anyone not previously in your list of contacts. If text messages are threatening in nature, tell a trusted adult and then keep screen grabs of the messages on file just in case. Then block the number. You can block individual phone numbers on many smartphones. If messages or calls keep coming in, ask an adult to contact the service provider. The service provider might advise you to file a police report. If you find yourself feeling anxious or depressed because of harassment, talk to an adult about seeking help from a counselor.

10 GREAT QUESTIONS

TO ASK A COUNSELOR OR THERAPIST

1. Why me?

2. What can I do when I feel like there's something wrong or different about me?

3. How can my parents help me to cope with bullying issues?

4. What should I do if I feel afraid at school?

5. How can I feel less alone and isolated?

6. What can I do if I'm feeling anxious or depressed?

7. What can I do if I feel threatened or unsafe?

8. How can I deal with extreme emotions, like anger?

9. What should I do if I'm experiencing suicidal thoughts?

10. What is the best way to break the bullying cycle?

Breaking Society's Cyberbullying Habit

As of 2019, all states have antibullying laws on the books. Some include antibullying policies to help schools deal with bullying. Some of these states have updated and improved their older antibullying laws to include cyberbullying. Although cyberbullying is a newer problem than regular bullying, it is getting increased attention from the government, schools, organizations, and the media.

LAWS AGAINST CYBERBULLYING

Making federal laws that help prevent cyberbullying is a tricky issue, partially because cyberbullying itself can be hard to define. Technology is constantly changing. In 2007, a federal cyberbullying law might not have included social media because it was not very widespread yet. Plus, in the United States the First Amendment of the Constitution protects people's rights to free speech and expression. If a cyberbully uses a racial slur against you, while it is extremely unkind and inappropriate, that person can't be arrested for it because his or her rights

Melania Trump speaks about her Be Best campaign at a 2018 antibullying event in Rockville, Maryland.

of free speech are protected. However, there are policies in place both at the state and federal level that can help protect you from long-term and emotionally damaging harassment. Parts of the Civil Rights Act of 1964 and the Americans with Disabilities Act operate to protect individuals who are facing certain types of discrimination in the workplace or at school. Bullying issues that aren't influenced by racial, LGBTQ, or sexual discrimination are handled under state laws.

Congress has considered laws that would make cyberbullying a federal crime. One bill, known as the Megan Meier Cyberbullying Prevention Act—named after a teen who died by suicide after facing long-term harassment online—has been before Congress in 2009 and 2010, but it has not passed into law.

Under specific state policies, schools can discipline students for bullying others online. In addition, some cities have made online harassment a crime.

Since 2010, public schools in New Jersey must follow the Anti-Bullying Bill of Rights. Some people think it is the strongest antibullying law in the United States. The law was created and passed, in part, because of Tyler Clementi, a student at Rutgers University's Piscataway, New Jersey, campus. Without asking permission, his roommate and another student used a webcam to spy on Clementi and another man kissing in his dorm room and then streamed the video online. Clementi died by suicide soon afterward.

SCHOOLS COMBATING CYBERBULLYING

In some states, teachers are required to report bullying. However, schools often have limited authority to handle cyberbullying if it occurs after school hours or off school grounds. If the cyberbullying is happening at school and is reported, school administrators will likely handle the situation. Counseling, whether by peers or guidance counselors or social workers, may be offered to the victim. If the cyberbullying escalates and becomes constant, the school may involve parents so that they can work to stop the behavior. The bullies could be suspended or expelled from school. In serious situations, the police might become involved.

Some schools provide ongoing programs that help create a healthy social climate while students are in school. Kids at every grade level are taught how to be leaders and to be concerned about others. They also teach people good ways of dealing with bullies.

Many schools are adopting bullying prevention programs provided by various organizations. One example is the Olweus Bullying Prevention Program, affiliated with Clemson Univer-

Speaking to a principal or school guidance counselor can often help to put a stop to cyberbullying. Know when to reach out for help!

sity in South Carolina. Schools in many different countries have used this program for several years. The program focuses on preventing or reducing bullying at the school, classroom, and individual levels.

Another example is the Anti-Defamation League (ADL). This organization works throughout the world to raise awareness of bullying through technology. The ADL stresses that schools should have clear policies on cyberbullying that include training for all staff. In addition, the ADL promotes bullying prevention laws in all states.

Through the organization Students Against Violence Everywhere (SAVE), students learn cyberbullying information and prevention. Then they practice what they learn about nonviolence and conflict management skills through school and community service projects. For more than ten years, Web Wise Kids (WWK) has taught students and parents about the dangers of using the internet and cell phones. WWK creates realistic and interactive computer games to reach teens and adults. To date, more than ten million middle and high school teens have been involved in WWK programs.

WHERE ELSE TO GO

The website StopBullying.gov of the US Department of Health and Human Services provides information from government agencies on how to prevent or stop bullying. It provides a list of resources for teens and their parents.

Sometimes, teens feel desperate about being cyberbullied and think they cannot talk to anyone. They may think about suicide because of their unbearable pain. Teens can call the National Suicide Prevention hotline any time, day or night at 1-800-273-8255. All calls are confidential. The specially trained staff provides immediate support by listening to callers and discussing their problems. If requested, staff can provide advice and tell teens where to go for more help. These hotlines are always open, and the call is free.

For LGBTQ individuals who are struggling, consider reaching out to the Trevor Project hotline at 1-866-488-7386, which is geared specifically toward the needs of those struggling with sexual or gender identity.

TAKING RESPONSIBILITY

Even though the internet may seem separate from the real world, there are rules about how to behave online. If teens break these rules, they could lose access to their social media

BULLY IN CHIEF

In 2018, First Lady Melania Trump announced her "Be Best" initiative, which, in part, would address issues with online bullying. According to Whitehouse.gov, "When children learn positive online behaviors early-on, social media can be used in productive ways and can effect positive change." However, the initiative has been controversial since it was unveiled because President Trump himself has been accused of using social media to bully others. Trump frequently shares, via Twitter, his feelings on individuals and organizations that have upset him. During the 2012 presidential campaign, he helped to promote the rumor that Barack Obama, the president at the time, was born outside of the United States. In 2016, when Trump was running for president, he tweeted, "President Obama will go down as perhaps the worst president in the history of the United States!" Many argue that some of his comments encourage others to engage in online or in-person harassment.

or other personal accounts. They could get into serious trouble with the law.

Teens should make sure all messages are kind and respectful. One way to do this is to avoid gossiping, passing on or starting rumors, or harassing others online. When a person is feeling upset or angry over a message he or she has received, it is a good idea for that person not to respond right away. Another idea is for teens to write a message and read it aloud to hear how it will sound to the reader. Or they can count to ten and read their message again. Before pushing the Send button, teens should try to picture the reader's reaction. They should not want the reader to feel angry, sad, or confused when seeing the message. In addition, teens should be careful before posting or sending messages or photos because those items could be used later by a bully to hurt them.

How each person acts online is critical. People might want to say mean things to others online, especially if they get upset over a rude or embarrassing message. Some teens may think it is fair to bully back. However, this reaction would only make

It's totally normal to feel a sense of guilt or anger when you've been the victim of bullying.

another cyberbully. Teens can fight cyberbullying by joining the antiviolence programs at their school, community center, local clubs, or religious organizations. If their school or community does not have a program, they could ask a teacher or guidance counselor to organize classmates into an antibullying group or club. Although raising awareness about cyberbullying must start with the individual, antibullying clubs can provide concrete information about the dangers of the internet, the effects of bullying, and effective ways to combat cyberbullies.

GLOSSARY

ANONYMOUS Not identified by name; of unknown name.

ASSERTIVE Having or showing a confident and forceful personality.

BLOCK To deny access. A person blocked from joining a chat usually receives a message that says access has been denied.

BULLYING Hostile behavior or intentional harm done by one person or a group, generally carried out repeatedly over time.

BYSTANDER A person who does not take part in an activity but watches or does not act to stop it.

CHAT An online conversation, sometimes carried out by people who use nicknames instead of their real names. A person can read messages from others in the chat room and type in and send in his or her own messages in reply.

CYBERBULLYING Intentionally harming somebody through electronic text or a technological device.

CYBERSTALKING Repeatedly following a victim around chat rooms, repeatedly sending emails or text messages, or calling a victim so that the victim feels there is no escape.

CYBER THREAT A message sent through the internet or a cell phone that is intended to inflict harm or violence on someone else.

EMAIL Electronic mail that allows internet users to send and receive electronic text to and from other internet users.

EXCLUSION The act of not including someone in an online group, such as a buddy list.

GAMER Someone who actively plays video games on a regular basis.

HARASSMENT Words or actions intended to annoy, alarm, or abuse another individual.

HOTLINE A telephone number that provides support for a particular type of problem.

INTERNET A worldwide network of computers communicating with each other via phone lines, satellite links, wireless networks, and cable systems.

ONLINE MULTIPLAYER Describing a type of video game in which players can log on to the game's server and participate with players all over the world.

SELF-ESTEEM Confidence in one's own worth or abilities; self-respect.

SOCIAL NETWORKING An online service that brings people together by organizing them around common interests, allowing them to share photos and chat with friends.

SPAM Unsolicited electronic mail sent from someone the recipient does not know.

TEXT MESSAGE A written message sent via an electronic device.

FOR MORE INFORMATION

BullyingCanada
27009-471 Smythe Street
Fredericton, NB E3B 9M1
Canada
(877) 352-4497
Website: http://www.bullyingcanada.ca
Facebook and Twitter: @BullyingCanada

This Canadian organization was created by young people and provides information and support to bullied youth.

Megan Meier Foundation
515 Jefferson Street
Saint Charles, MO 63301
(636) 757-3501
Website: https://meganmeierfoundation.org
Facebook and Instagram: @meganmeierfoundation
Twitter: @MeganMeierFndn

The Megan Meier Foundation teaches children, parents, and educators about the prevention of the bullying and cyberbullying of youth.

PACER's National Bullying Prevention Center
8161 Normandale Boulevard
Bloomington, MN 55437
(888) 248-0822
Website: http://www.pacer.org/bullying

Facebook: @PACERsNationalBullyingPreventionCenter
Instagram: @pacer_nbpc
Twitter: @PACER_NBPC

PACER's National Bullying Prevention Center unites, engages, and educates communities nationwide to address bullying through creative, relevant, and interactive resources. This organization has named October the National Bullying Prevention Month.

SAVE (Students Against Violence Everywhere) Promise Club
(866) 343-7283
Website: http://www.nationalsave.org
Facebook: @NationalSAVE
Instagram: @nationalsave
Twitter: @NATIONALSAVE

This public nonprofit organization strives to decrease the potential for violence by engaging students in violence prevention efforts within their school and community.

StopBullying.gov
US Department of Health and Human Services
200 Independence Avenue SW
Washington, DC 20201
(877) 696-6775
Website: http://www.hhs.gov
Facebook: @StopBullying.gov
Instagram: @stopbullyinggov
Twitter: @StopBullyingGov

StopBullying.gov provides information from various government agencies on how children, teens, parents, educators, and others in the community can prevent or stop bullying.

The Trevor Project
PO Box 69232
West Hollywood, CA 90069
(310) 271-8845
Website: https://www.thetrevorproject.org
Facebook: @TheTrevorProject
Instagram: @trevorproject
Twitter: @TrevorProject

The Trevor Project is a national organization dedicated to crisis intervention and suicide prevention services for LGBTQ individuals under the age of twenty five.

United States Department of Justice
950 Pennsylvania Avenue NW
Washington, DC 20530-0001
(202) 514-2000
Website: http://www.justice.gov
Facebook: @DOJ
Instagram: @thejusticedept
Twitter: @TheJusticeDept

The United States Department of Justice provides information about cyberbullying and federal leadership in preventing and controlling crime.

FOR FURTHER READING

Borba, Michele. *UnSelfie: Why Empathetic Kids Succeed in Our All-About-Me World.* New York, NY: Touchstone, 2016.

Craft, Jerry. *New Kid.* New York, NY: HarperCollins, 2019.

Dawson, Juno. *This Book Is Gay.* Naperville, IL: Sourcebooks, 2015.

Halloran, Janine. *Coping Skills for Kids Workbook: Over 75 Coping Strategies to Help Kids Deal with Stress, Anxiety and Anger.* Eau Claire, WI: PESI Publishing & Media, 2018.

Hemmen, Lucie. *The Teen Girl's Survival Guide: Ten Tips for Making Friends, Avoiding Drama, and Coping with Social Stress.* Oakland, CA: Instant Help, 2015.

Hitchcock, J. A. *Cyberbullying and the Wild, Wild Web: What You Need to Know.* Lanham, MD: Rowman & Littlefield, 2016.

Jennings, Jazz. *Being Jazz: My Life as a (Transgender) Teen.* Toronto, ON: Ember, 2017.

LaCour, Nina. *Hold Still.* New York, NY: Penguin, 2019.

Mardell, Ashley. *The ABC's of LGBT+.* Coral Gables, FL: Mango, 2016.

Mayrock, Aija. *The Survival Guide to Bullying: Written by a Teen.* New York, NY: Scholastic, 2015.

Phillips, Alexandra. *Click: A Story of Cyberbullying.* Berkeley, CA: Zuiker, 2018.

Raja, Sheela, and Jaya Raja Ashrafi. *The PTSD Survival Guide for Teens: Strategies to Overcome Trauma, Build Resilience, and Take Back Your Life.* Oakland, CA: Instant Help, 2018.

Siwa, JoJo. *JoJo's Guide to the Sweet Life: #PeaceOutHaterz.* New York, NY: Abrams, 2017.

Skeen, Michelle, and Kelly Skeen. *Just as You Are: A Teen's Guide to Self-Acceptance and Lasting Self-Esteem.* Oakland, CA: Instant Help, 2018.

Soerens, Matthew, Jenny Yang, and Leigh Anderson. *Welcoming the Stranger: Justice, Compassion & Truth in the Immigration Debate.* Westmont, IL: IVP, 2018.

Toner, Jacqueline B., and Claire A. B. Freeland. *Depression: A Teen's Guide to Survive and Thrive.* Washington, DC: Magination Press, 2016.

Wolk, Lauren. *Wolf Hollow.* New York, NY: Puffin, 2018.

BIBLIOGRAPHY

Anderson, Monica. "A Majority of Teens Have Experienced Some Form of Cyberbullying." Pew Research Center, September 27, 2018. https://www.pewinternet.org/2018/09/27/a-majority-of -teens-have-experienced-some-form-of-cyberbullying.

Brooks, David. "The Cruelty of Call-Out Culture." *New York Times*, January 14, 2019. https://www.nytimes.com/2019/01/14 /opinion/call-out-social-justice.html?rref=collection %2Ftimestopic%2FCyberbullying&action=click&content Collection=timestopics&region=stream&module=stream_unit &version=latest&contentPlacement=1&pgtype=collection.

de Moraes, Lisa. "*The View* Calls on Melania 'Be Best' Trump to End Donald's Attacks on John McCain and Grieving Family." Deadline, March 20, 2019. https://deadline.com/2019/03 /the-view-melania-donald-trump-john-mccain-be-best-attack -meghan-cyberbully-1202579066.

Ducharme, Jamie. "More Kids Are Attempting and Thinking About Suicide, According to a New Study." *TIME*, May 16, 2018. http://time.com/5279029/suicide-rates-rising-study.

Hathaway, Jay. "What Is Gamergate, and Why? An Explainer for Non-Geeks." Gawker, October 10, 2014. https://gawker .com/what-is-gamergate-and-why-an-explainer-for-non -geeks-1642909080.

Holson, Laura M. "Instagram Unveils a Bully Filter." *New York Times*, May 1, 2018. https://www.nytimes.com/2018/05/01 /technology/instagram-bully-filter.html?rref=collection %2Ftimestopic%2FCyberbullying&action=click&content Collection=timestopics&region=stream&module=stream_unit &version=latest&contentPlacement=4&pgtype=collection.

Kelly, Emma. "What Happens When You Become a Meme? Overly Attached Girlfriend and Ermahgerd Girl on How It Changed Their Lives." Metro.co.uk, July 31, 2018. https://

metro.co.uk/2018/07/31/happens-become-meme-overly
-attached-girlfriend-ermahgerd-girl-changed-lives-7782212.

Klass, Perri. "In the Fight Against Bullying, a Glimmer of Hope."
New York Times, August 28, 2017. https://www.nytimes
.com/2017/08/28/well/family/in-the-fight-against-bullying-a
-glimmer-of-hope.html?rref=collection%2Ftimestopic
%2FCyberbullying&action=click&contentCollection=timestopics
&region=stream&module=stream_unit&version=latest
&contentPlacement=9&pgtype=collection.

McCammon, Sarah. "One Month Later, What's Become of
Melania Trump's 'Be Best' Campaign?" NPR, June 7, 2018.
https://www.npr.org/2018/06/07/617642736/1-month-later
-whats-become-of-melania-trumps-be-best-campaign.

Milbank, Dana. "One Easy Trick for Melania Trump to Reduce
Cyberbullying." *Washington Post,* August 20, 2018. https://
www.washingtonpost.com/opinions/while-one-trump-warns
-against-cyberbullying-the-other-is-perfecting-it/2018/08/20
/dbab7778-a4b8-11e8-97ce-cc9042272f07_story.html?utm
_term=.ee6cedf24bf2.

PACER's National Bullying Prevention Center. "Cyberbullying."
Retrieved March 22, 2019. https://www.pacer.org/bullying
/resources/cyberbullying.

Scheff, Sue. "Can Technology Curb Cyberbullying?" *Huffington
Post*, October 12, 2017. https://www.huffingtonpost
.com/entry/can-technology-curb-cyberbullying
_us_59de7b58e4b069e5b833b1fc.

Stephen, Bijan. "Another One of Jennifer Lawrence's Hackers Is
Going to Prison." The Verge, August 30, 2018. https://www
.theverge.com/2018/8/30/17800896/jennifer-lawrence-hackers
-prison-celebgate.

Trump, Melania. "Be Best." The White House. Retrieved March
22, 2019. https://www.whitehouse.gov/bebest.

INDEX

ABOUT THE AUTHORS

Pam T. Glaser faced her own bullies growing up. She decided that writing about bullying would help her better understand her bullies and her own experiences. She writes frequently about issues for teens and lives in Omaha, Nebraska.

Judy Monroe Peterson has earned two master's degrees and is the author of many educational books for young people. She is a former health care, technical, and academic librarian and college faculty member; a biologist and research scientist; and curriculum editor with more than twenty-five years of experience.

PHOTO CREDITS

Design & Layout: Brian Garvey; Editor: Bethany Bryan; Photo Researcher: Sherri Jackson